VULCAN & HIS TIMES

VULCAN
& HIS TIMES

PHILIP A. MORRIS

Published by

BIRMINGHAM
HISTORICAL SOCIETY

With the support of the Susan Mott Webb Charitable Trust,
the Greater Birmingham Foundation, the Alabama
Historical Commission, Time Warner, Inc,
Vulcan Materials Company Foundation,
Philip A. Morris, and Robinson Iron.

Front cover illustration: Cast of iron in Birmingham, Vulcan served as the Birmingham and Alabama exhibit for the 1904 St. Louis World's Fair. As god of the forge, he holds a spear point he has just made on his anvil. The sculptor was Italian-born Giuseppe Moretti. Missouri Historical Society WF 1035; photographer: Dept. of Mines & Metallurgy, 1904, St. Louis, MO.

Title page illustration: A formal portrait of the upper portion of the plaster cast of Vulcan was taken in the partially built St. Stephen's Church in Passaic, New Jersey, used by sculptor Moretti as a studio. This photograph, published on the front page of The Birmingham News *on January 30, 1904, also appeared in newspapers across America. Here Moretti leans back above his skilled crew while press agent James MacKnight stands at lower left. Birmingham Public Library Archives.*

Back cover illustration: Rear view of Vulcan today includes the change from gray paint to a brick red color applied to represent the iron ore seam from which he came. Photographer: John O'Hagan, 1995.

ISBN 0-943994-20-9
Library of Congress 95-81571

The Birmingham News

THE BIRMINGHAM AGE-HERALD

PREFACE

In the fall of 1903, industry in Birmingham and in the entire nation, was in full bloom. The Birmingham District was proven as a major producer of iron and had begun to produce steel rail. Iron foundries were prevalent. U. S. Pipe had begun the manufacture of cast iron pipe; other companies such as Acipco and McWane would follow. A process of consolidation had started. Virginia interests had acquired the Sloss ironmaking facilities. Republic Steel had purchased the Thomas furnaces. U. S. Steel would shortly acquire the Tennessee Coal, Iron and Railroad Company (TCI). Barely 30 years old in 1903, Birmingham was a success, ready for recognition, and anxious "to make its attractions known to men of capital, brains and enterprise who should be drawn to the [area's] wonderful fields of opportunity . . ."

The opportunity to advertise Birmingham to the nation and the world with an exhibit at the 1904 St. Louis World's Fair was presented to the Commercial Club (predecessor of the Chamber of Commerce) by James MacKnight, a journalist and promoter. MacKnight suggested a sculpture of iron, the largest in the world, as an appropriate means of attracting "wide attention . . . to the colossal mineral wealth of Alabama . . . and to symbolize Alabama's supremacy in the production of iron." The State of Alabama being without the means to produce

This photomontage, entitled "Birth of a Birmingham Pig," shows the various stages of pig iron production at Birmingham's Woodward Iron Company — from mining the ore within Red Mountain (top left) to tapping the furnaces and casting the pig iron (bottom right). The photograph appeared in The Birmingham News-The Birmingham Age-Herald *on July 24, 1938 as the Vulcan Monument on Red Mountain was nearing completion. At this time Birmingham was America's leading foundry ironmaker. Birmingham Public Library Archives; photographer: C.A. Cassady, Technical Photograph Company; photographed by John Acton.*

a major exhibit, it fell to the Commercial Club, as the representative of industry in the Birmingham District, to organize and finance the exhibit. Already prominent, the Commercial Club increased its membership during the period of its sponsorship of the World's Fair exhibit. Important members included James Bowron, Secretary of TCI; F. M. Jackson, coal operator; A. B. Loveman, department store executive; Robert Jemison, promoter of the nation's second largest street-car railroad; and Rufus Rhodes, editor and publisher of *The Birmingham News*. These were men of pluck and get up and go, accustomed to challenge and success.

In the art world, it was a period of heroic sculpture. Frederic Bartholdi's Statue of Liberty was completed in 1886. Large statues were frequently commissioned for homes and public parks, and especially for world fairs. For their heroic statue, the Commercial Club chose a most unheroic figure: Vulcan, the Roman god of the forge, a working man, usually pictured in sooty, dirty surroundings, engaged in hard labor. Perhaps because he reflects the reality of the Birmingham District, rather than unwordly mythology, Vulcan has been a popular sculpture through the years, with an image appealing to the common man. In the 1950s he was one of the few tourist destinations in Birmingham, drawing as many as 250,000 visitors a year. Certainly, Vulcan was a success in 1903 and 1904 when his picture appeared in newspapers in the major cities of the United States and around the world, frequently on the front page. It may be that the city has never again experienced such favorable publicity as it did during 1903 and 1904, as the world was introduced to Vulcan, the symbol of Birmingham's success.

Preserving Vulcan for Birmingham remains a challenge. Not until the 1930s was Vulcan installed in an appropriate place on Red Mountain overlooking the Birmingham District. Today, Vulcan is in need of significant repair and improvement to the park surrounding him. The challenge presented is to marshall the same measure of civic pride and community spirit that moved the Commercial Club to create Vulcan in the first place, so that he can continue his work as symbol of our city and region.

Marjorie L. White

TABLE OF CONTENTS

INTRODUCTION

Standing high above the valley where he was poured from molten iron in 1904, Vulcan speaks eloquently but silently of time and place and people. The shadow cast by his distinctive form reaches the length of Birmingham's history. This monumental Roman god of the forge, set atop a ridge named for the iron ore within, combines setting, art and symbol into a unique American landmark.

They often do not know his name, but visitors who have seen Vulcan profiled in the sky above Red Mountain never forget. The statue has that most affecting image, the human form, but of colossal size — 56 feet from sandals to outstretched hand. Elevated above the ridge on a 123-foot-tall column, the ensemble has heroic presence unusual in this country.

Memorable as he is, Vulcan is not well understood. An example: the spear point he has made and holds up for all to see is hidden under the wrap of a traffic fatality light. The god of the fiery forge holds — a Popsicle?

Lost to memory, too, is the saga of Vulcan's creation as Birmingham's exhibit at the St. Louis World's Fair of 1904, the controversy about where to put him upon his return to Birmingham, his sad days at the fairgrounds and his eventual placement on Red Mountain.

This book hammers into a tight format a concise and fact-filled history of Vulcan and the times he has seen. As you will discover, he has always been more than just a statue — even if the largest cast iron sculpture in the world and the largest U.S. statue after the Statue of Liberty in New York harbor. He embodies the spirit of place, ambivalent and changing over the years. Even now, as the weathered giant needs mending and the city embraces an industrial history long ignored, fresh meaning is here to be uncovered.

Vulcan, of course, has always been "uncovered" in part, revealing his position within a classical art tradition. For all his weighty seriousness, he's made generations of grade-schoolers titter and grown people smile. Just so, these stories of his creation and endurance, condensed from many sources and carefully researched newspaper reports, will both convey facts and evoke emotion.

Aloof as he may seem, Vulcan lives among us and shares our being in this place.

Opposite page: Vulcan was triumphant when finally placed atop his pedestal on Red Mountain in the late 1930s. The Birmingham News - The Birmingham Age-Herald, *July 24, 1938, photographer: C.A. Cassady, Technical Photography Company.*

THE BIG IDEA

For Alabama and the South, Birmingham at the end of the 19th century was certainly an upstart.

Minerals for a promising future had lain underground for eons, but mapping of the resources came only in the mid-1800s, and railroads connecting the sparsely settled area to distant markets only after the Civil War. After its founding in 1871, the newly planned industrial town struggled with a cholera epidemic, the national financial panic of 1873 and other setbacks. But by the 1880s, growth began in earnest and, by 1900, this out-of-nowhere "Magic City" had become the state's largest with a population of more than 38,000, not counting the soon-to-be-consolidated suburbs of Woodlawn, Ensley and Pratt City and other settlements across the emerging Birmingham District.

The boomtown attracted entrepreneurs from Alabama and nearby states, and also from far afield. Among them was James A. MacKnight, a widely traveled Salt Lake City native with a diverse career in journalism, foreign service and promotion. He came to Alabama from New York City for health reasons, failed at establishing a central Alabama colony for northerners and, by 1902, had assumed management of the Alabama State Fair.

Building on contacts made in that position, MacKnight, by early 1903, was floating the

By 1900, industrial-boomtown Birmingham had become the largest city in Alabama and one of the fastest growing in the nation. In this 1908 view looking north on 20th Street toward Capitol Park (now Linn Park) with the First National Bank (now Frank Nelson Building) on the right, skyscrapers were bursting above the late-19th century street scale. Alvin Hudson Collection.

idea of an Alabama exhibit for the Louisiana Purchase Exposition (World's Fair) to be held in St. Louis in 1904. He had visited the 1876 U.S. Centennial Exposition in Philadelphia, happened to know key players in the planned St. Louis event, and felt the state's little-known resources deserved wider exposure.

BIRMINGHAM SIGNS ON

Failing to generate state interest by late summer of 1903, MacKnight found a sympathetic response from two officers of Birmingham's Commercial Club (predecessor to the Chamber of Commerce): F.M. Jackson and J.B. Gibson. Jackson, a native of Hamburg, Alabama, who had risen quickly in Birmingham industry and at this time served as president of the organization, became particularly important to the project. On October 13, despite skepticism from some members — especially about the short lead time — the club approved MacKnight's concept of a Vulcan exhibit and agreed to raise the estimated $15,000 ($220,000 in today's dollars) to carry it out.

Outlandish as a giant statue of Vulcan in iron seemed to some members, to others it was just the right thing. "Robert Jemison (Sr.) said that he thought Alabama would have an advantage over any other state making an exhibit because the iron man would be so unusual and conspicuous," stated a newspaper

In this view of the St. Louis World's Fair of 1904, the Palace of Mines and Metallurgy is visible on the left, with a grand entry flanked by a pair of giant obelisks. Most fair buildings were temporary structures, their exteriors covered in staff (a tough plaster). Birmingham Public Library Archives.

Vulcan, being the Roman god of the forge, was included in the classical themes pursued in art beginning with the Renaissance. Here, the muscular Vulcan is shown at his forge by Flemish painter Hendrick Van Balen. In classical tradition, the gods were draped, but seldom clothed. Venus at the Forge of Vulcan, *based on a work by Jan Brueghel, the Younger (1568-1625), John Woodman Higgins Armory, Worcester, MA, photographed by Don Eaton.*

report on November 7th. From the start, organizers planned for the statue to be returned to Birmingham and set up in Capitol Park (now Linn Park) as a permanent work of civic art.

Key support was also enlisted from Gen. Rufus N. Rhodes, editor and publisher of *The Birmingham News*, who printed frequent editorials first championing the idea and then generating needed financial underwriting. A November 9 editorial stated: "The big statue of Vulcan at the Louisiana Purchase Exposition will suggest the solidarity of the Birmingham district. It's a good idea and cannot fail to make a hit."

Exposure at the St. Louis fair was seen as advertising and promotion for the industrial district, and viewed by more visionary business leaders as a way to attract new manufacturers to Alabama. Instead of shipping raw metal north to be turned into products, they felt the city needed to develop home markets, adding jobs and dollars to the economy. At Vulcan's feet would be exhibits of the state's raw materials and products made from them. Though international fairs in this period did provide amusement, great emphasis was placed on presenting goods and resources. (The Palace of Mines and Metallurgy, where the Birmingham exhibit was allotted 2,000 square feet of floor space, covered nine acres.)

Vulcan In Mythology

In ancient Roman mythology, Vulcan stood out for being useful. Born of Jupiter and Juno, he was, depending on the account, thrown from Mt. Olympus by his mother because he was lame and ugly, or by Jupiter because he sided with Juno in an argument. After falling a whole day, he landed on a Mediterranean island and, assisted by the Cyclopes, worked his forge of volcanoes to produce shields, weapons and chariots for the gods. In point of fact, most Birmingham voices raised in his support referred more to the colossal presence of "the big iron man" than to his Roman roots.

Monumental sculpture paired with grand classical architecture in the Beaux Arts manner had become a feature at recent fairs. The enormous Statue of the Republic and a life-size figure of a woman in silver representing Nevada at the magnificent World's Columbian Exposition in Chicago (1893) together helped plant the seed for the Birmingham proposal, one combining heroic size with local product.

Logical, but barely established, was the tie between Birmingham ironmaking and Vulcan, the Roman god of the forge. An early instance of Vulcan as a local symbol is found as an industrial supply company advertisement in an 1886 book promoting the city. And for Birmingham's Mardi Gras celebrations, held from 1896 until 1899 (when recurring cold weather caused their cancellation), the king was named "Rex Vulcan."

MacKnight's initial concept was a large figure cobbled together from various raw materials and products across the state. But by the time the idea came before the Commercial Club, it had jelled as a colossal Vulcan 45 feet tall. He described the quick evolution in a newspaper column several months later:

An 1886 book promoting the region, The Mineral Wealth of Alabama and Birmingham Illustrated, *contains this advertisement, the first-known local use of what appears to be a figure of Vulcan, though not identified as such. Birmingham Historical Society.*

In the early interviews between Mr. Gibson [Commercial club secretary] and the writer, the project was far less ambitious than the sequel would indicate. We first figured on building a crude figure of colossal dimensions out of steel billets, pig iron, and fragments of coal, ore and lime rock. My familiarity with the art world told me that a statue in iron, such as could be created as a work of art, would cost more money than we could raise, and that at least a year would be needed to make the models. But by the time the project was submitted in August, all other designs had been eliminated, and I had determined that a colossal work of art was the only thing that would 'fill the bill.' (Birmingham Age-Herald, February 28, 1904)

More ambitious, indeed. MacKnight made his first trip to St. Louis officially representing Birmingham and the Commercial Club on October 19, 1903, where he received positive response and, eventually, an improved location for the exhibit. But worry about the timetable seemed justified as MacKnight, traveling by train across the Northeast, began to seek out a sculptor for the job. His letter to the club in mid-November reported that the prime candidate, Cyrus Dallin of Boston, assured him, "that such a statue would require two to three years to make, and anyone who thought it could be done in less time was off the rails."

The Louisiana Purchase Exposition would open April 30, 1904, just over five months away, and MacKnight had not yet found an artist who would accept the challenge.

Sculptor Giuseppe Moretti, in a portrait with a miniature model of Vulcan, was in his mid-forties when he accepted the Birmingham commission, a physically demanding project that Moretti executed with unheard-of speed. Hannah Elliott Collection, Birmingham Public Library Archives.

In the years prior to Birmingham's Vulcan, Moretti had created major public monuments in Pittsburgh, including the 56-foot-tall Welcome, *the gates to Highland Park. Mercer Papers, Birmingham Public Library Archives.*

MORETTI TO THE RESCUE

Then MacKnight found Giuseppe Moretti. An Italian-born sculptor with his studio in New York City, Moretti had recently completed major civic works in Pittsburgh where industry connections may have led MacKnight to him. Moretti was experienced in bronze and iron casting and, at this time, associated with the J. L. Mott Iron Works in New York.

Born in Sienna, Italy, Moretti had studied in Florence, practiced in Austria-Hungary and emigrated to the United States in 1888. An accomplished artist then in his mid-forties, he was vigorous and quick. The challenge of

Moretti Biography

Born in Sienna, Italy in 1859, Giuseppe Moretti was the nephew of an Italian cardinal and art patron. The young Moretti first studied art with the monks of San Domenico and, later, at the Academy of Fine Arts in Florence. After an initial career in Austria (frustrated by nationalist politics), he emigrated to the United States in 1888, receiving his first American commissions from architect Richard Morris Hunt for statuary and friezes at the W.K.Vanderbilt Residence, Newport, RI and work on the base of the Statue of Liberty.

Though his studio was located in New York City from 1888 to 1904, his major work during the 1890s consisted of monumental bronze statuary for Pittsburgh parks under parks director Edward Bigelow.

Prior to the Vulcan commission, Moretti had won a bronze medal at the Paris Exposition of 1900 for a smaller work, *The Angel and the Book of Life* and, in 1903, completed a statue of Cornelius Vanderbilt erected at Vanderbilt University in Nashville. While in Alabama, Moretti became enthusiastic about Sylacauga marble, sculpting a head of Christ exhibited at the St. Louis World's Fair of 1904 and, in 1908, a memorial statue of teacher Mary Cahalan commissioned by Birmingham Mayor George Ward and now located in Linn Park.

In 1909, Moretti returned to Italy, but was soon back in the U.S. creating World War I memorials for a number of cities and commissions for influential patrons across the Northeast. From 1916 to 1923, his studio was in Pittsburgh. Moretti returned again to Italy in 1925 where he died at San Remo in 1935 at the age of 76.

creating a great Vulcan sculpture appealed to both his artistic and entrepreneurial spirit. In negotiations, the $2,000 artist fee established for the project was raised to $6,000 (about $87,000 in current dollars). For that, the Commercial Club secured both talent and can-do enthusiasm. Moretti would make a clay model, create a full-scale plaster cast, come to Birmingham to oversee casting in iron and then supervise installation in St. Louis.

The Birmingham News reported a contract was signed on November 24. About the same time, the *New York Herald* ran a front-page feature and Moretti's sketch of Vulcan. The publicity for Birmingham that MacKnight promised had already begun. Within a two-week period, an eight-foot model in clay was completed in Moretti's New York studio, described by an observer: "The model represents a bearded figure with a leather apron, one arm extended high over its head holding a trion and the other resting on a stump." The latter became an anvil in final form.

Initial reports stated the full-size plaster model would be made at Thomas A. Edison's Laboratory near West Orange, New Jersey, but Moretti settled, instead, on an unfinished church in Passaic, New Jersey, just across the river from New York City. With 16 assistants, he began translating the model into monumental scale.

Meanwhile, on December 4, *The Birmingham News* introduced the sculptor to the local population with a short biographical column written by MacKnight and run under a stacked headline typical of the day: *"MAN WHO WILL MAKE THE COLOSSAL VULCAN • G. Moretti, a Native of Italy, a Lover of America • WHY HE CAME TO THE UNITED STATES • Wished to Make His Home Where No Foreign Power Could Dictate • Some of His Magnificent Productions in Bronze and Marble • DOING BIRMINGHAM A SERVICE."*

Also on December 7, a mass meeting was called to generate public support for the project. Jefferson County had committed $5,000, but the fundraising had only just begun even as the first clay was being shaped onto a great wooden armature by Moretti and his assistants.

Moretti first made a 24-inch model of Vulcan in clay for approval of the Commercial Club. He then created an eight-foot-tall model from which he and his assistants created the full-size plaster model with upper and lower halves. Unlike the final version, this model stands on a mound (of minerals) and has a tree trunk rather than an anvil. Other differences are also evident. Birmingham Public Library Archives, photographed by John Acton.

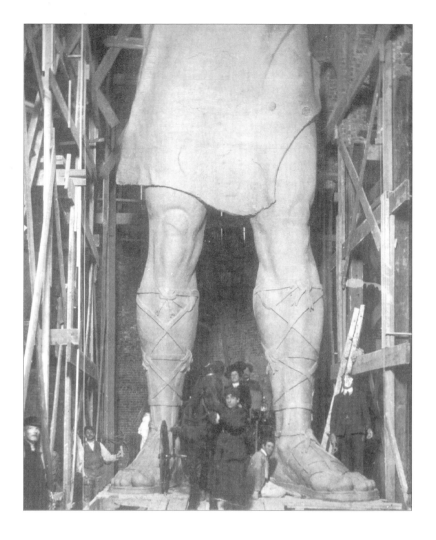

VULCAN SHAPES UP

The first image showing city residents the size and character of what was to be a 56-foot-tall Vulcan — a photograph from the waist down with workmen at his feet — appeared in the *Birmingham Age-Herald* on January 9, 1904. It may have given the impression that the statue was formed first in plaster, but the initial step was modeling in clay. Due to the weight of the clay, a full-length model would have collapsed of its own weight. Moretti executed Vulcan in lower and upper halves, so he first saw the completed work when assembled in St. Louis.

The national press played the story big, just as MacKnight predicted and probably helped promote. The *New York Sun* ran a major feature and the *Chicago Tribune* a full-page spread with illustrations on February 14, 1904 (see illustration).

An excellent account of the procedure and speed with which it was accomplished appeared in the *New York World*, on February 11:

The enormous scale of Vulcan, as shown in this photograph of the lower half in the New Jersey church/studio, caught the imagination of the national press. A carriage is shown passing between Vulcan's legs. Early in 1904, this photo was published by newspapers in New York and Chicago. Library of Congress Lot 9901; photographer: A. B. Bogart.

Moretti, the sculptor, of 152 W. 38th Street, has just completed the plaster cast. One of the most interesting things about the work is the brief time given the artist to complete it. He began his life-size clay model in November. He did not get started on the colossal figure until December.

He employed a number of workmen to build an armature, or framework of wood, according to measurements, for the enlargement. The first section was from the soles of the feet to the waistline, being 29 feet high. The width across the hips was 10 feet and 6 inches. The clay was then laid on this framework, and the work of modeling begun.

The Chicago Tribune *published this "picture page" on February 14, 1904. The caption beneath the Vulcan model read:* "The Vulcan Model Entire Primitive Man Triumphing Over Nature in the Discovery of Giving Iron a Keen Edge (Producing Steel)," *Chicago Public Library.*

In the ordinary course of statue building, the work on this section would have required a year or more. Mr. Moretti completed it in a month, and had the plaster cast made in the following manner. When he completed the modeling in clay, which he did entirely with his own hands, he had the big clay figure covered with a thick coat of plaster of Paris, which was toughened, and held together with strips of burlap.

This coating of plaster, when it set, became a perfect matrix of the figure. It was carefully removed in sections, so the wood work and clay could be taken away. The matrix was then set up, and bound together with iron bands to support the plaster, which was in turn poured inside of the mold, producing the feet, legs, and body to the waist.

The head, arms and upper body are now undergoing a similar treatment, in the new Church of St. Stephen at Passaic; and shipment of the parts to Birmingham has begun.

Though this account implies such, the plaster model was not solid. The plaster matrix was assembled around a space-consuming core, leaving the inside hollow. Similar steps would be used in making the iron castings. Confusion about the modeling and casting process is evident in an article in the *Birmingham Age-Herald*, January 26, where, under the headline, *"VULCAN PLASTER CAST WILL ARRIVE THIS WEEK,"* the text says, *"The giant clay model has been covered with a heavy coating of plaster of Paris. It will be cut into sections for shipment to Birmingham."*

MacKnight, in a January 22 letter to the Commercial Club, reported the excitement about both the size and artistic quality of Vulcan generated by visitors viewing the work. His writer's skill shows in this still-vivid portrayal of the then-plaster giant: *"A full-sized man could be buried in one of the beautiful feet of the colossus, and a company of four could sit down to luncheon in his head. Two men could lie at full length inside of his right arm, and a dainty dancer might do her stunt on the nail of his giant toe."*

Dimensions of Vulcan

The original claim that Vulcan is the largest cast metal statue in the world appears to hold true. At 56 feet high, Vulcan claims this title over the 37-foot-tall bronze Buddha figure created in Kamakura, Japan, c.1252. He also stands tall as the second largest statue in the U.S., a distant second to Frederick Bartholdi's 151-foot-tall Liberty Enlightening the World in New York Harbor. Liberty is made of hammered copper over an iron framework. Vulcan's vital statistics, actually projections made prior to casting, were published by the *Birmingham Age-Herald* on March 13, 1904:

Total height — 56 feet

Height to top of head — 51 feet

Length of face — 7 feet, 6 inches

Length of foot — 6 feet

Length of arms — 10 feet

Distance across shoulders — 10 feet

Circumference of chest — 22 feet, 9 inches

Circumference of waist — 18 feet, 3 inches

Estimated weight of figure — 100,000 pounds

Weight of anvil block — 6,000 pounds

Weight of spear head — 350 pounds

Weight of hammer — 300 pounds

Further claims made for Vulcan by John Henley, Jr., with his 1938 publication, *Birmingham's Vulcan*, stretch his monumental presence: "Vulcan stands atop a pedestal 124 feet high, so that the monument, as a whole, rises to a height of 179 feet, which is taller than Niagara Falls. Since the statue was planted on the crest of a mountain some 390 feet above the center of the city it overlooks, Vulcan surveys Birmingham from an elevation of nearly 600 feet, just over the height of the Washington Monument, the tallest shaft in America."

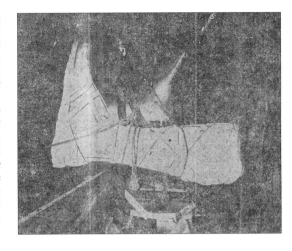

PARTS ARRIVE IN BIRMINGHAM

The Foundrymen's Challenge

"It was decidedly the hardest casting ever made in Birmingham, and it taxed the ability of the foundrymen. Several who have visited the foundry have stated that they would never have known how to go about it," reported the *Birmingham Age-Herald*, April 25, 1904, as the final work commenced. In a 1962 interview in *The Birmingham News*, 82-year-old Fred Buettiker, the last remaining molder of Vulcan, said the men worked 60 hours a week for four months at 35 cents an hour. During the last six weeks, Buettiker, who had started foundry work at age 14, did not leave the plant at all, with castings made at 2 a.m. or anytime they were ready.

Winter weather hindered both completion of the plaster casts and their shipment via railroad flatcars. Extreme rain and cold in the unfinished church studio caused some plaster work to freeze and collapse, so parts of the upper portion had to be reworked.

On February 12, *The Birmingham Age-Herald* headlined, *"FIRST INSTALLMENT OF COLOSSAL VULCAN HERE."* The report noted, *"The car, which is thirty-six feet long, contains the portion of the statue from the waist to the knee, which weighs about 8,000 pounds. . . . It was eleven days on the flat car exposed to the snow, wind and rain, and there are only one or two places where it is at all damaged."*

That same day, *The Birmingham News* reported that a contract to cast Vulcan into iron had been let to Birmingham Steel and Iron Co., newly established by W.T. Adams (of Corinth, Mississippi) and J.R. McWane to take over the former Hood Machine and Foundry Co. including its equipment. The company's bid was very low, an estimated 25-to-50 percent below what any other firm would have submitted. The foundry was small and newly reorganized. And the castings would be more difficult than anyone could have guessed. The race against the calendar would only get more difficult.

The act of pouring an iron casting took only minutes, but the steps leading up to it were arduous and time-consuming. The size and intricacy of the parts would challenge even Birmingham's best foundrymen who were recruited to the foundry for this job.

Work on making molds from the plaster model began on February 15. Though the concept was the same as making plaster casts, these molds were to be made of brick and loam in order to withstand molten iron. Vulcan would be assembled out of 15 large pieces — feet and lower legs, upper legs and hips, waist, chest and back, etc. — bolted together internally. But these castings would require fabrication of many more mold components, or drawbacks, which were shaped against the plaster and baked until hard. These would then be put together in sections for casting the parts.

On February 16, the *Birmingham Age-Herald* reported, *"The active work of casting the Vulcan will commence today or tomorrow. In order to make the castings, the Birmingham Steel and Iron Company had to dig a large hole in the center of its shops on 14th Street and First avenue (North) into which the moulding will be placed."* In fact, the first casting was not poured until March 12. Elaborate preparations needed for each casting were not fully grasped.

As parts were being laboriously molded, others were arriving, often delayed by bad weather in transit. Simultaneously, the lagging fundraising to pay for it all had to be pushed by the Commercial Club with special events and appeals. The fund to date had less than $10,000, and final cost would top $20,000 (an estimated $280,000 in today's dollars), considerably more than predicted.

The Chianti Factor

Any shock that Italian immigrant Moretti might have encountered with the culture of 'frontier' Birmingham was eased by the fact that he brought his own culture with him. His personal chef also served as chief critic for the sculptor and, together, they made a big impression. A feature article published in the *Birmingham Age-Herald* soon after they arrived commented: "Moretti is also an excellent cook. He is said to possess a fine baritone voice and is not averse to singing when occasion demands. He is a very temperate man, rarely drinking anything stronger than the native Chianti, which might be said to comprise his principal article of diet."

This section of a 1902 Sanborn map pinpoints where Vulcan was cast on the south side of First Avenue North at 15th Street. In 1904, J.R. McWane and W.T. Adams formed Birmingham Steel and Iron Co. and purchased the Hood Machine Co. foundry, one of many foundries and mills that then marched through the Birmingham city center along the Railroad and Mechanical Reservation. A close look reveals two breweries nearby (lower left), not uncommon in pre-prohibition days. William Stanley Hoole Special Collections Library, University of Alabama, Tuscaloosa, AL.

The Molding Process

Not only was the making of the molds for the iron casting of Vulcan's various parts extremely hard to do, it is also difficult to describe. Around the particular plaster cast being worked on, molders would simultaneously manipulate a layer of loam following the exact shape of the piece and an outer layer of brick. Segments would be marked for position and then slightly separated and baked hard. They were then assembled in position to make the core for the hollow center. To do this, the interior surface of the mold was plastered with sand to the desired thickness of the casting (from 3/4 inch to 2 1/2 inches). While the wet sand was being applied, the brick core was built against it. When the core of a casting was complete, the mold segments were again disassembled, the sand removed, and the segments replaced again. The entire outer mold and inner core structure was then dried and lowered into a pit, reinforced from the outside and then poured. Metal filling the thin space between mold and core would solidify into the hollow iron casting. This is virtually the same process employed today in lost-wax casting, in which wax is substituted for the sand.

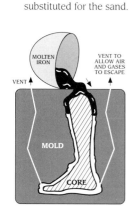

The pouring of the iron took only minutes, but the making of the complicated molds from brick and sand took weeks at the hands of skilled foundrymen. This drawing roughly outlines the cavity between the outside mold and the interior core where the iron would be poured. Illustrator: Scott Fuller.

"ONE SECTION OF VULCAN," the title over this photograph read when published in the Birmingham Age-Herald *on March 16, 1904. There were 15 major pieces cast to make up Vulcan. As casting proceeded toward the opening of the world's fair on April 30, fundraising moved slowly. Birmingham Public Library Archives; photographer: Bert Covell; photographed by John Acton.*

CASTING AND FUNDING RACE

Moretti arrived on February 18 and lived up to the image of an artist, though not a temperamental one. "I greatly enjoy it here," he told the press. "You see, I am used to the smoke and the dirt, for I frequently go to Pittsburgh, but the climate is my delight." He traveled with two assistants and his private chef. He opened a temporary studio across First Avenue North from the foundry.

To boost funding and public interest, an event was scheduled February 26 at the Jefferson Theater, including a solo sung by Moretti. The fund had reached a total of $12,238.50 by the next day. On March 4, the *Age-Herald* published a photograph showing a plaster cast of a foot and leg being lifted from the second freight car to arrive, weeks late, from New Jersey.

The newspaper's multi-line headline of March 11, just over a month-and-a-half away from the fair's opening, summed up the dual push for Vulcan: *"FIRST CASTING TO BE MADE TODAY • About 3 o'clock the Iron Will Commence Running • Money is Badly Needed • Many Plans Being Tried to Get Funds for the Expenses of Vulcan • New Ones Suggested."*

On hand for this first casting were the core-makers and molders, George Rush, Nick Smith, J. T. Sorsby, Fred Buettiker, Henry Stepp, Charles Zward, Ike Swanson, Henry Veitch and many others, plus distinguished visitors that included Moretti, Jackson and Gibson. Also present were Barney Conlin, foreman of the foundry and owner James R. McWane.

Photographs of the casting process were not feasible due to smoke, but the first part completed — the hips and upper legs weighing about 12,000 lbs. — was reported a success. Polishing and smoothing rough edges began. Except for the immediate painting to prevent rust, Moretti told the gathering that Vulcan was being done in the same manner as a cast bronze statue.

Casting of the second piece (seven feet tall from waist to below the armpits), also using about 12,000 lbs. of metal, followed on March 16, and a third was reported made on March 19. "This new portion cast consists of the two legs from about six feet below the waist to the knees. It is covered in the front by the apron of Vulcan, and the entire piece was cast at the same time," a newspaper reported. This section took 10,000 lbs. of molten iron.

Next came the lower legs and feet. They were to be two inches or more thick to carry the weight of the statue, compared to the head

Vulcan Fund Contributors

Pledges to the Vulcan fund came quickly at the start of the campaign. Jefferson County's initial $5,000 contribution served as the lead gift, with others following in modest increments ranging from $1 to $500. The United Mine Workers' gift was among the first and largest at $500, with the same amount coming from the Sloss-Sheffield Steel and Iron Co., Tennessee Coal and Iron Co. and Birmingham Belt Railway Co. Contributing $300 each were First National Bank and Alabama Consolidated Coal and Iron Co., with $200 from Blocton-Cahaba Coal Co. and $100 each from Birmingham Fertilizer Co. and Bessemer Fire Brick Co. The press announced these pledges February 11, 1904, with many smaller ones listed and many more to come.

Due to the intricate detail, the most difficult part to mold and cast was Vulcan's head. This retouched photograph (smoke made photography at the foundry difficult), showing the construction of the brick-clad mold being made for the head, ran in the American Machinist *on July 6, 1905. The Library of Congress.*

One $5 contribution came from Paris, France, given by a Mrs. Mary McLeary who identified herself as a Birmingham property owner.

As costs for the statue and exhibit increased substantially beyond original estimates, Vulcan fundraisers would employ then-innovative strategies to pay for Vulcan, including art shows, concerts, baseball games, statuette sales, and passing the hat at corporate offices and among Commercial Club members. In the end, owners of the Birmingham Steel and Iron Company would substantially reduce their bill, making the foundry the second largest financial contributor to the estimated $20,000-$25,000 fund.

In the same time period, newspaper accounts record that $100,000 was much more easily raised for the new charity hospitals, Hillman and St. Vincent's, and $40,000 for the YMCA building fund.

which would be about three-quarters of an inch thick. Though it was to have taken place on March 20, the right leg and foot segment were not poured until the 26th. Work proceeded round-the-clock, but the push could not offset the unusual preparation needed. On March 22, the press reported that Charles L. Ledbetter, one of the best foundrymen in the city, had been brought into the project to help move it to completion.

"The casting of the right foot and leg of Vulcan as high as the knee was probably one of the most successful castings ever made in Birmingham," reported the *Birmingham Age-Herald* on March 27. "It required about 12,000 pounds of iron to make the casting and the metal flowed as smoothly as could be desired. It was an exceedingly hard casting to make, owing to the peculiar shape of the mold, the amount of metal required and the size of it."

In the meantime, a benefit baseball game featuring the New York Giants and pitcher "Iron Man" Joe McGinnity (known for his ability to pitch double-headers and his work as a foundryman in off-season) playing the Birmingham Barons (then the "Coal Barons") on March 23 raised over $600. The Vulcan fund was still below $15,000.

Also published in the American Machinist *1905 article was this photograph of the completed casting of Vulcan's head, which weighed approximately 15,000 lbs. Library of Congress.*

At the Commercial Club meeting on April 1, Jackson was re-elected to an unprecedented second term as president in recognition of his efforts on Vulcan. The next day, Vulcan's chest, the smallest piece at 8,000 lbs., was cast, and molding on the shoulders began soon after.

A portion of the work crews was now engaged in fitting the pieces together to be sure they could be assembled without problems in St. Louis. Because some parts contracted more than others, the flanges intended to hold the parts together had to be adjusted.

On April 13, the casting of Vulcan's shoulders (14,000 lbs.) was successfully completed, but the most difficult part of all — the head — was still underway. The plaster cast had been dropped and damaged earlier in March, but Moretti quickly made repairs and molding began on March 28. Created without a top to minimize weight, the head's intricate features took special care. The mold was baked to extra hardness to prevent any features of the face being spoiled in the casting. The intricate curls of the beard were particularly difficult, and Moretti was on hand to supervise every move.

Meanwhile, the first Frisco railroad car loaded with Vulcan's feet and legs left for St. Louis on April 18, the original deadline to have the entire sculpture on site. Other parts followed, but the troublesome head would not leave Birmingham until May 8. To complete the job, Williamson Foundry pitched in to cast the final small pieces. When the St. Louis fair opened to the public with great fanfare on April 30, there was plenty to see, but not much yet of Vulcan.

MEET ME IN ST. LOUIS

"THOUSANDS ADMIRE THE GREAT STATUE OF VULCAN," read the *Birmingham Age-Herald* headline on May 1, 1904, but their admiration could only reach as high as his knees. *"Several parts of the statue are already in place, and this exhibit is attracting more attention than any other one thing in the exposition. . . People stood for an hour at a time studying the outlines of the legs to the knees and the piece immediately above the knees,"* the reporter said (with, it must be assumed, some exaggeration).

Moretti arrived in St. Louis in early May to supervise assembly and apply finishing touches, including application of a cement mixture to smooth some rough seams. The same dark grey paint, applied to the metal at the foundry to prevent rust, disguised the

The Fair Was Late, Too

Vulcan wasn't the only late-comer. To mark the 100th anniversary of the Louisiana Purchase, the St. Louis World's Fair should have opened April 30, 1903. But organizers realized early on they could not make that date, so the exposition was "dedicated" on that date and opened a year later. Attractions spread over 1,240 acres drew an average 100,000 visitors per day. Like most temporary fair structures of the era, ornate palace exteriors were shaped from staff (reinforced plaster). One permanent structure was the core of the Palace of Fine Arts, now part of the St. Louis Museum of Art. Vulcan, the great "Iron Man" from Birmingham, AL, remains one of the few other large, surviving artifacts of the fair.

Little Vulcan Souvenirs

Both for fundraising and for souvenirs, the Commercial Club contracted with a Connecticut firm to produce 2,000 Vulcan statuettes in bronze, 12 inches tall. An earlier attempt to cast them in iron proved unacceptable. The *Birmingham Age-Herald* noted on June 2, 1904: "Many ladies are purchasing two of them and placing them at either end of the mantels in their homes." Sales were also brisk at the fair.

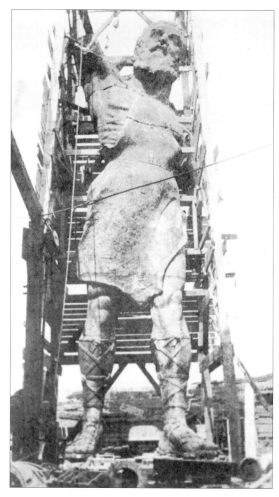

Birmingham's first view of Vulcan at full scale came in late April with assembly of the plaster casts supported by a scaffold at the Birmingham Steel and Iron Co. foundry. Only the front was fully visible. Birmingham Public Library Archives; photographer: G. M. Cushing, Boston.

Statuettes like this one were sold in Birmingham and at the St. Louis fair to help defray costs of creating Vulcan. Statuette courtesy Gwyn Turner, Demopolis; photographer: Will Dickey.

patching. Several bolt holes had been omitted in the rush to ship parts from Birmingham, so even as installation was reported complete on May 25, last-minute work had kept exhibits at Vulcan's base from being completed.

Back in Birmingham, the fund was still $4,000 short of its goal. On May 18, the plaster cast of Vulcan, tinted to resemble the iron version, went on view outside the Birmingham Steel and Iron foundry. A twenty-five-cent admission charge intended to raise money was soon removed. President Jackson decided the club could generate more income selling statuettes. The 12-inch-tall cast bronze replicas of Vulcan produced by the Commercial Club were selling well at $2 each, with proceeds going to the fund.

When Vulcan, which the fair had declared the official Alabama exhibit, was dedicated on June 7, all was in order. Vulcan towered over everything in view within the Palace of Mines

and Metallurgy, with exhibits from 20 Alabama counties spread at his feet. Given the fact that the statue's site measured only 32 x 62 feet, the heroic scale of Vulcan stole the show. The polished steel spear point in his hand almost touched the roof. Vulcan was christened with a bottle of Cahaba River water when Miss Miriam Jackson, representing reform forces trying to turn Birmingham away from drink at the time, refused to use champagne for the purpose.

During the run of the St. Louis World's Fair (extended to December 1, 1904), nearly 20 million visitors came. There were eight major exhibit palaces and acres of diversions ranging from the newly invented automobile to a tribe of pygmies, but Vulcan unquestionably stood out. More than 20,000 visitors signed the exhibit register and Vulcan statuettes sold out.

Only Vulcan's feet and lower legs were in place when the St. Louis World's Fair opened on April 30, 1904, but by dedication in early June, the "Iron Man" was triumphantly dominating the huge Palace of Mines and Metallurgy. Exhibits at his feet featured raw materials and products from 20 Alabama counties. Fair officials named Vulcan the official Alabama exhibit, and an international panel of jurors awarded him a grand prize. Lettering on the anvil's base reads, "Vulcan God Of Fire & Metals — Cast At — Birmingham, Alabama." Missouri Historical Society WF 1035; photographer: Dept. of Mines & Metallurgy, 1904, St. Louis, MO.

Paired images placed in a stereoscopic viewer were popular in 1904. These served as fair souvenirs. Library of Congress Lot 11043-4; photographer: Keystone View Company Stereograph No.15176, Meadville, PA; St. Louis; San Francisco; Toronto; New York; London.

When an international panel judged the mineral department in September, they awarded Vulcan the Grand Prize and gave medals to Moretti for sculpting and James R. McWane for casting him.

Near the fair's end, officials from San Francisco offered to purchase Vulcan for a price considerably more than he had cost. But

Another view at the fair of Vulcan up to his waist shows the exit to the Alabama exhibit, and Vulcan's exposed rear. The finish resembles nickel steel, rather dark and lustrous. Moretti supervised the final installation at the fair, smoothing over some rough joints with a cement mixture tinted to the same nickel steel patina. Library of Congress Lot 11041-4; photographer: Keystone View Company Stereograph No. 15175.

even before he was complete, on May 10, the Commercial Club had passed a resolution donating Vulcan to the community with certain stipulations:

> *Resolved. That the Commercial club of Birmingham hereby tender this great statue as a free gift to county of Jefferson and the city of Birmingham on conditions that it shall be erected in Capitol Park at the head of Twentieth Street, north, at the expense of said county and city, but under the direction of the Commercial club; the statue to be erected as soon as possible after its reception in Birmingham.*

The club's presumption that this was a good idea would be challenged.

HOME TO CONTROVERSY

After the fair, Vulcan was disassembled by a St. Louis storage company and, in February 1905, transported back to Birmingham free of charge by the L.&N. Railroad. In October, the Commercial Club had settled on a final price for casting Vulcan. Birmingham Steel and Iron reduced its $10,070 bill by $2,400 because it was a "public enterprise," and, at its November meeting, club members voted to assess themselves to pay off the $4,000 balance not covered by the public fundraising. However, the question of remaining debt was not resolved until spring. As controversy about the chosen

Capitol Park, later Woodrow Wilson and now Linn Park, was surrounded by houses of leading families, as this photograph taken in 1900 indicates. With beautification recently completed, women objected to putting Vulcan in the park. Wilson Scrapbook, Birmingham Public Library Archives.

location in Capitol Park bubbled through the community, Vulcan was hauled in March 1905 to a site on Red Mountain along the L.&N.'s Mineral Railroad where he lay in pieces for 18 months. Beggs Foundry recast the Iron Man's right arm as it had been broken during transit from St. Louis.

To understand resistance to putting Vulcan in Capitol (now Linn) Park, a picture of Birmingham at that time is helpful. The city begun at the railroad crossing was growing rapidly, and the first 'skyscraper' — the 10-story Woodward Building — had been erected at 20th Street and First Avenue North. But six blocks away, the park (named on the vain hope that the state capitol would be moved there) was a late-19th-century residential square surrounded by houses of the city's elite. Fountains, curving walkways, and flower beds had been developed, and the obelisk commemorating the Confederacy had recently been erected (1902). The mighty statue, so ruggedly impressive in the Palace of Mines and Metallurgy, was aesthetically unacceptable here. Though there was no public mention about the prospect of his exposed posterior looming above ladies strolling and children playing, it must have been the talk of the neighborhood.

Already, some felt the proper place for Vulcan was Red Mountain, and this site where Vulcan "would be visible for miles around" was promoted by Dr. J. W. Stagg, pastor of First Presbyterian Church. Mayor George Ward, who had encouraged organization of women's groups to pursue City Beautiful improvements for the city's neighborhoods, also favored Red Mountain.

But, as Raymond Rowell describes in his *Vulcan in Birmingham* (published on occasion of the city's centennial in 1971), two votes were soon held, and both strongly favored Capitol Park. First, the Commercial Club called for a vote of all those who had given to the Vulcan fund: one vote for each dollar given. The county cast its 5,000 votes for the park, the city its 500 for Red Mountain. The totals were 8,716 for Capitol Park and 2,165 for Red Mountain. About two weeks later, on March 21, Birmingham City Council voted 11 to 4 in favor of Capitol Park.

"Delegations of women, heads of clubs, and almost anybody 'who didn't have anything to do that week' descended on City Hall," Rowell's account reads. *"Vulcan suddenly became a 'menace' to public health, decency, and Birmingham's 'culture.' The Council soon*

Is Vulcan Ugly?

When Fred Buettiker, a foundryman who helped make the molds for casting Vulcan in 1904, took his new wife from Tennessee to see Vulcan close up, she remarked: "Who ever made an ugly thing like that?" It was many years before he told her he had worked on the project, reported the *Birmingham Age-Herald* in a 1946 interview with Buettiker and another original molder. From inception, the question of Vulcan's lack of comeliness was present. Some members of the sponsoring Commercial Club felt he should be more graceful and attractive, but sculptor Moretti held firm to his position that a proper likeness required a figure that was rugged and — if not actually ugly — not at all like Adonis or Michelangelo's David. In addition, the deliberate distortion used by Moretti (making the head 2 1/2 feet larger than normal so it would have the proper scale when viewed from below) left the completed work open to criticism. Aesthetic estimations, of course, vary by era and personal view. Moretti shaped an honest image of the god of the forge at work, although some sensibilities would have preferred a ballet master.

rescinded its popular 'decision,' and the matter of location again lapsed into status quo; or something similar."

The truth is, the women and Mayor Ward were on solid critical ground. A colossus, even one fully clothed, was overscaled for the modest block-square park and the houses around it. Many thoughtful people felt the still-undeveloped ridge just south of the city was a natural location. Miss Alice Rumph, commenting to the press, said it perfectly: "It seems to me that Red Mountain — the source of Vulcan — is the proper site." And it would be, but not for a very long time.

TOO LONG
AT THE FAIR

On September 15, 1906, a *Birmingham Age-Herald* story reported the Commercial Club pushing for a final disposition. "It is the desire of the club to get rid of Vulcan at once so that the entire energies of the organization may be devoted to other objects." Vulcan remained a dismembered refugee just a little longer until Commercial Club member J. A. Emery approached the president of the newly reorganized Alabama State Fair Association about erecting Vulcan at the fairgrounds in

As a temporary solution to the controversy about where in Birmingham to erect Vulcan, he was erected in the fall of 1906 at the state fairgrounds in Birmingham's West End. This view, made about 1910, has him towering above the crowd with the race track visible to the right. Birmingham Public Library Archives; photographer: O. V. Hunt.

Vulcan's left hand, installed incorrectly and unable to hold his hammer, was soon put to use hawking products, the first an ice cream cone. Birmingham Public Library Archives.

This profile view indicates Vulcan's upraised hand installed incorrectly and a timber supporting his lower arm. Birmingham Public Library Archives; photographer: W. P. Gaines.

Birmingham (same site as the present fairgrounds in Birmingham's West End where surrounding residential areas were then under development). Seen as a temporary move, Vulcan would remain there nearly 30 years.

With the fall fair of 1906 just a few weeks away, it was arranged for Vulcan to be transported on the Birmingham and Bessemer Railroad, a local streetcar line. The route from Red Mountain was circuitous and included a ride through downtown Bessemer. Since Vulcan was under two years old, the management drolly ruled, Vulcan got to ride free.

This was another rush job. Vulcan arrived at the fairgrounds on Saturday, October 13, and assembly began on Sunday, the day before the fair opened. This time, without Moretti to supervise, the workers mounted his hand backwards so Vulcan was unable to hold his spear point. Rowell reports that the spear point lay on the ground for the decades Vulcan would spend at the fairgrounds. His left arm was also misaligned so that its supporting hammer was not reinstalled. Instead, a timber was used to support the arm, adding to the awkward appearance.

He was not assembled properly, but at least Vulcan was up, visible to the local public for the first time. "The men working on the big statue accidentally dropped Vulcan's hand. . . This has been doctored and the big fellow is now intact," reported the *Birmingham Age-Herald* on October 19. As in St. Louis, he towered over the fair, and during his long stay there, he served an impromptu, but important, lost-and-found function. Children were told by parents, "If you get lost, go to the feet of Vulcan and we will find you there."

"The idea of moving Vulcan to the fair and allowing the people of the state and the South an opportunity of seeing how he looks on foot is still the subject of favorable comment," the press reported. And, no doubt, for generations of children who played at his feet, the memories of the giant iron man were fond ones. But this visibility was limited to just a few weeks a year, and the carnival atmosphere of the event

Here, Vulcan is used to promote Heinz 57 pickles. Birmingham Public Library Archives.

A July 1936 Birmingham News *photograph shows Vulcan painted flesh color with contrasting sandals. Mercer Papers, Birmingham Public Library Archives; photographer: Alfred Jacob.*

soon pulled the god of the forge into an embarrassing huckster role.

Entrepreneurs found a use for Vulcan not at all god-like — or even dignified. Reportedly, the first to take the opportunity was the Weldon Ice Cream Company which had a stand nearby. They had a huge ice cream cone fabricated of plaster and chicken wire and placed in Vulcan's left hand — the one meant to hold the hammer — which now hawked the company's product (see photographs).

This commercial use was unplanned, but by about 1914, fair authorities began selling the spot as advertising space. An ad for Heinz pickles later occupied the spot, but the longest-running one was a Coca-Cola bottle. At some point during the 1920s (not documented), Vulcan was disassembled and lay on the ground for some years, most likely due to structural problems. In the early 1930s, he was reerected, painted flesh color, given black eyebrows and rouged cheeks. About this time, he was used to advertise locally produced Liberty overalls — by wearing the largest pair ever made.

Little wonder, then, given the sad state of what had been conceived as a noble symbol for Birmingham and its work in forging metal, that a movement soon began to re-dignify Vulcan by putting him where he truly belonged, overlooking the city from Red Mountain.

1935: Vulcan Pro and Con Letters

After plans to move Vulcan to Red Mountain were announced, certain artists and architects attacked the idea in the press. Other citizens wrote letters to the editor for and against the city's symbol. A sampling of opinions follows:

I have had the good fortune to see some of the best and ugliest sculpture in Europe and America and I would, without hesitation, give the booby prize to Pretty Boy Vulcan. In fact, it never occurred to me until I read your editorial that this ugly, badly designed and badly proportioned monstrosity was anything but a circus attraction, and that anyone should want to move him from the Fair Grounds to a place in the sun where more people can see him only to laugh — well, that just calls for a law against it. Max Heldman

Mr. Heldman's attitude toward Vulcan seems singularly devoid of feeling for a comrade who has rejoiced and suffered with the people of Birmingham for a great many years . . . For despite Vulcan's alleged ugliness (and indeed, what symbol of 'rugged individualism' ever was artistic?), there are few among us who have not at some time or other felt a kinship with the God of Fire. His life has been similar to our own: crammed with alternate events of joy and despair . . . As to the symbolism of Vulcan being as outmoded as the horse and buggy, would that indicate he should be destroyed? On the contrary, we need to retain a little of the old as temper for the new. Wm. J. Tucker, Jr.

RED MOUNTAIN REVIVAL

Maybe it was the painting of Vulcan to look something like a clown that was the final straw, but in the summer of 1935, a committee of the Birmingham Kiwanis Club led by Tom Joy and Mercer Barnett went public with a plan to move Vulcan to a Red Mountain site. They had done their homework and made a compelling presentation to the Birmingham Parks and Recreation Board on July 25. A major news feature on the proposal published July 28, 1935, stated: *"The site on which the committee wishes the monument located is 75 feet above the Montgomery Highway, the prospectus shows. It provides that Vulcan be mounted on a high pedestal. The figure, it says, is 55 feet high and the monument would be visible from all over Birmingham and Shades Valley."*

Back during the 1906 controversy, the same location was reportedly promised as a site for Vulcan by the owner, Tennessee Coal Iron and Railroad Company, at the request of the Cadmean Circle, a socially prominent women's literary organization. But now, there were many more factors in favor of success. To begin with, active mining of iron ore in this section of the mountain had ceased and the mineral railroad just below the site with a trestle bridge across the highway cut had seen its last official use in 1933 (It was on this line that

Vulcan had been delivered to a nearby site when he returned from St. Louis in 1905).

The shift from industrial extraction to urban development had begun just east of here in 1909 when Jemison & Company and Willis J. Milner employed well-known landscape architects to lay out premier residential areas such as Valley View, Altamont Parkway, Redmont Park and Milner Heights. Major ore deposits were removed in advance of development.

Accessibility, which would have been a major issue in 1906, was about to be enhanced by four-laning the federal highway over the mountain. At this time, U.S. 31 (the Montgomery Highway) was the only all-paved highway in the state. In fact, the Alabama Highway Department had been lined up as a major partner in the project by also agreeing to extend roadways up and into the park site.

And, as of September 1923, when a Birmingham parks department was created by state law, there was an agency to oversee and operate the proposed development. A citywide parks plan prepared by the Olmstead Brothers firm (designer of the New York City and Boston park systems) and published by the board in 1925 had called for a linear park following the crest of Red Mountain. The plan was not followed, but it had included the site now designated as Vulcan Park as part of a 480-acre mountain-top park which was planned to extend west to the current George Ward Park.

The Birmingham Parks and Recreation Board voted on August 28, 1935, "to request the City Commission to secure a site for 'Vulcan' and park on the crest of Red Mountain from TCI&R Co., if possible." Meanwhile, the other — and, by far, the most crucial — partner in the project was being courted: the Depression-era Works Progress Administration (WPA). It would take four years to the official dedication, but Vulcan was going home to his red ore source on the mountain.

WPA COMES THROUGH

Birmingham, with a population of 320,000, was hard hit by The Great Depression due to reliance on heavy industry. Though major WPA projects in the area, intended to create immediate jobs and foster economic revival, were new sewer lines and development of an industrial water system, the more visible improvements

Opportunities to have portraits made with Vulcan's parts prior to reassembly were taken by many. Tower scaffolding is visible at right. Birmingham Public Library Archives; photographer: Albert Benham.

were those made to parks. Approved in October of 1935, the official WPA funding for Vulcan included a federal grant of $39,874. The project, officially entitled, "Moving and Erecting of the Vulcan Statue," WPA Project No. 37-1465, was estimated to employ 114 men for six months.

A resolution passed by the park board January 8, 1936, noted transfer by gift of the 4.5-acre site to the City and the WPA grant covering all costs but design and road construction. The Birmingham architectural firm of Warren, Knight and Davis was commissioned to prepare plans and specifications, though the park board stated clearly that no funds for the design were currently available (The firm would be paid a total of $3,175 in eight installments.).

Groundbreaking for Vulcan Park was held the third week of February 1936. On hand to turn the first shovel of dirt was F. M. Jackson, the business leader who saw the original Vulcan effort through to completion. The Kiwanis Club, with Tom Joy pushing the current work in similar fashion, received a letter of congratulation from Leila MacKnight, the widow of James MacKnight.

But not everyone praised the move. Controversy again swirled through the community, mainly via the letters-to-the-editor section of the newspapers. Some thought it a waste of money, while certain members of the art community felt Vulcan did not merit such prominence. It may have been just a tempest in a teapot, but the commentary provides an illuminating debate about Vulcan's artistic and symbolic character (see letters).

The architects' preliminary design for the monument called for a formal Beaux Arts column in smooth stone ornamented with carved

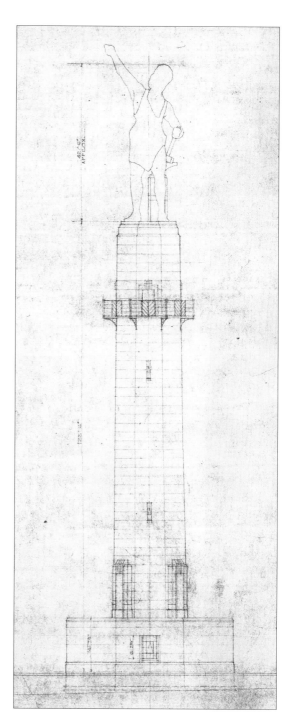

This 1936 drawing for the "Vulcan Monument on Red Mountain for the City of Birmingham," projects a tower with an open-air balcony. Warren, Knight & Davis, Architects, Courtesy Robert M. Black Architects, Inc.

stone sculptures at the base. As built, it evolved into a taller, simpler and more slender 123-and-a-half-foot octagonal tower, slightly tapered and averaging 20 feet in diameter. Constructed of reinforced concrete, the tower would be clad in rusticated stone of the sort employed for many WPA park structures in Birmingham and elsewhere. A small museum was to be included at the base.

The 160 steps inside the column led to a three-and-a-half-foot-deep open-air balcony with a chevron railing detail that gave it an Art Moderne turn. From the platform, visitors would have views of Vulcan immediately above, the city to the north and suburban ridges and valleys to the south. Counting the Red Mountain ridge and the tower, Vulcan would reach nearly 600 feet above the valley floor of the city, a truly monumental scope for the statue.

Also participating in the design process was Birmingham parks superintendent R.S. Marshall, who conducted a topographic survey and helped develop the site plan. A newspaper report included his assessment: *"It is the roughest four and one-half acres I ever surveyed. There is a difference of 97 feet in the elevation of the highest and lowest points in the park. There are some old mine openings on the north edge of the property and a lot of waste from the old mine in which big trees have grown. Although it is rough, it can be made a beautiful park."* Marshall also noted that there was enough native red stone on the site to build walls and walks.

No drawings of site improvements (other than those of the architects for the tower and of the tax assessor for other park structures) have been located, and it is not clear who designed the layout of the cascades, retaining walls, walks and other features. Joy, who was trained as a civil engineer, may have shared this responsibility with Marshall.

The new Vulcan Road led up from the Montgomery Highway to a 100-space parking lot. Straight ahead toward the base of the tower was a double walkway with four pairs of steps centered by a three-tiered, 42-foot-wide cascade, the water tumbling by gravity over rough stones. From the base of the monument, a system of walks extended outward along the crest. Two sets of stone steps, one facing the city and the other fronting the highway, provided access for pedestrians from streetcar stops below.

What distinguished the WPA-era design was the emphasis on using native materials (as had been done with local iron for Vulcan) and the high level of handcraft exhibited. The project proceeded in seemingly slow motion, like the general economy. But the subtle fit with the landscape meant Vulcan would be truly at one with the mountain.

HOME AT LAST

Concrete for the tower foundation was poured mid-April 1936. Parks superintendent Marshall told the press, *"To obtain a perfect foundation we moved the location of the monument 8 feet*

Italian Stonemasons' Art

Put to work by the WPA crafting stonework for Vulcan Park were many Italian immigrant stonemasons who also worked on fine residences along Red and Shades Mountain in flush times. Carlos Mazarra served as foreman for the crew, named on a bronze plaque placed in the park in August 1937 by the Italian-American Progressive Association. The pink sandstone used to face the column holding Vulcan was quarried not far away at Lane Park, the quarry now incorporated into the Birmingham Botanical Gardens Kaul Wildflower Garden. The 1993 report on Vulcan Park by the Historic American Engineering Record (HAER) describes the now-concealed WPA stonework thusly: "Exterior surfaces consist of irregularly coursed, rectangular, quarry-faced, originally pink (now light brown) sandstone blocks." Though modern features completed in 1971 have obscured much stonework, the site retains the greatest concentration of stonemason's art at any Birmingham public facility.

south. *Borings with a diamond drill show that the foundation will rest on a heavy ledge of rock from 10 to 12 feet thick, and then below that clay and more rock. We drilled down 68 feet to be sure that we had an absolutely strong foundation. The last 28 feet was solid rock."* A particular concern was mines running under the site. (The opening to the former Lone Pine Mine No. 3 was incorporated into the walkway system. Strip and underground mining had taken place here in 1904 and 1907.)

"Vulcan being moved to Red Mountain this week," read the Kiwanian newsletter a few months later on August 25. "Much favorable publicity has greeted this civic enterprise sponsored by our club. . . Much credit for the success of this project goes to Tom Joy who worked tirelessly on the preliminary plans and now daily visits the job to advise with the project superintendent on the various engineering problems in connection with the work."

On November 12, 1936, Vulcan's right leg was hoisted to the top of the completed tower preceded by a formal ceremony attended by representatives of the Kiwanis Club, the Chamber of Commerce, city, county and the parks board. When the statue was erected up to the thighs, the first round of 120,000 pounds of concrete was poured inside to stabilize it before the upper parts were installed, newspapers reported. At this time, 50 men were reported at work on the project.

A newspaper photograph published April 11, 1937, when well-known economist Stuart Chase visited the site, showed Vulcan up but still surrounded by scaffolding. By early May, the scaffolding was removed and Vulcan was fully visible from Red Mountain. He had been cleaned and finished with aluminum paint to increase visibility.

On October 31, the *Birmingham News-Age Herald* ran a major feature on Vulcan and his new park setting, with accompanying photographs suggesting construction was complete. But work on the interior of the museum at the base, to be clad in white marble from the Sylacauga quarries that had impressed Moretti, only began in March 1938. The road leading into the park was being prepared for paving.

There were also problems deciding how to illuminate the statue. It was finally determined to mount four poles, each holding four 1,500-watt floodlights a distance of 150 feet from the tower

Vulcan is just visible atop his tower through scaffolding surrounding both tower and statue in this photograph, published April 11, 1937, by The Birmingham News-Age Herald. *Birmingham Public Library Archives; photographer: J. Edwards Rice; photographed by John Acton.*

Trumpeters announced Vulcan's Queen during the dedication pageant on Red Mountain in May 1939. Birmingham Public Library Archives.

as well as mounting smaller floodlights at the top of the column immediately below the statue. A dedication date was tentatively set in October 1938, but this was pushed back to the following spring. Reasons for the delay are not clear.

Finally, the finishing touches on Vulcan Park were complete and a nine-day schedule of events beginning May 7, 1939, would mark the official dedication. The Chamber of Commerce organized the festivities. There was a contest for a Vulcan Queen to preside, and a popular swell of support elected Miss Evelyn Tully of Wylam who worked at a downtown cosmetics counter. Rain postponed the opening vespers service. The next night, leading industrialist Erskine Ramsey crowned the queen with her 24 ladies of the court standing near.

A crowd of 5,000 was on hand for the ceremony and the attendant spectacle — a historical pageant in eight acts. Several performances were cancelled due to rain, but the show — with a cast of 1,200 directed by William Baker of New York and featuring the young George Seibels, Jr.(Birmingham's future mayor), as Vulcan — did go on. The acts, in order, were: "Vulcan at his Forge with the Dance of Fire, Working on the Armor for Achilles; Coming of the Spaniards; the Arrival of the Pioneers; Birth of Birmingham, the Calico Ball of 1873; the Gay Nineties; and Gesture Toward the Future with all the court and young women dancing as 'men of steel'; Indians, conquistadors, explorers, pioneers and settlers as they appeared in the pages of Alabama history."

Vulcan's Queen, Evelyn Tully, was elected by popular vote. Birmingham Public Library Archives.

Guests of honor at the events included James MacKnight's widow and men involved in the casting of Vulcan: Clarence Hancock, George Rush and Fred Buetticker. Vulcan had found his place in local history and was now to become the city's number one visitor attraction. He had newfound prestige as a symbol of the city. Nobody compared Red Mountain to Mt. Aetna (site of Vulcan's forge in ancient times), but Vulcan was up with the sky and clouds.

SYMBOL CHANGES MEANING

In his new, highly visible location on the ridge overlooking Birmingham, Vulcan was revived as a worthy symbol of the city. The number of local companies using "Vulcan" in their name jumped (see sidebar). And as promoted in the campaign to move him, Vulcan quickly became a popular destination, this in a city lacking visitor attractions. The Birmingham Museum of Art, Birmingham Zoo, Birmingham Botanical Gardens and other civic institutions did not yet exist.

This photograph of Vulcan and Vulcan Park, which won a Chamber of Commerce competition, captures the superb fit the WPA-era stonework provides between the monument and its prominent natural setting. Birmingham Public Library Archives; photographer: O.V. Hunt.

In 1941, Tom Joy arranged for donation of the George H. Clark Collection of Alabama minerals which became the principal exhibit for the museum at the base of the tower. This was intended to be the nucleus of a first museum for the city of Birmingham (The valuable collection disappeared from the site during subsequent renovation.).

Visitors in the 1930s approached the recently completed Vulcan monument along this series of cascading pools. Stonework came from a quarry now part of the Birmingham Botanical Gardens Kaul Wildflower Garden. Birmingham's Vulcan, *1938.*

The location of Vulcan Park on U.S. 31, the main north-south highway through Birmingham and Alabama, also facilitated visitation and brought Vulcan to the attention of out-of-state travelers, many headed from Nashville and the midwest to Florida. The widening of the highway coordinated with creation of the park was part of a federal- and state-sponsored Good Roads program intended to encourage automobile tourism.

Though the advent of World War II interrupted the growth of tourism, the park, with its colossal statue, was like nothing else. And for those ready to climb the 160 steps in the monument, the open-air observation platform 25 feet below Vulcan offered a stunning view of the statue, and of the city environs below.

Installation of a traffic safety light in 1946 covered a replacement spear point, which is still underneath. Birmingham Public Library Archives; photographer: Watson McAlexander.

It was an automobile-related initiative that soon deprived Vulcan of his essential symbolism. In 1946, the Birmingham Jaycees safety committee came up with the idea of turning his upreached arm into a traffic safety beacon. Though intended to be temporary, the green/red light remains to this day. With a more permanent installation, the spear point Vulcan holds was wrapped in a metal cone and fitted with neon tubes. The light stays green unless someone has been killed in traffic, when it turns red for 24 hours. For generations

Motoring visitors approached the Vulcan monument from this parking lot. Upon reaching the top of the cascades and the tower, the visitors stepped outside to a panoramic view of the city, and of Vulcan. Birmingham's Vulcan, 1938.

After the road up to Vulcan was extended in the early 1950s, the Red Mountain crest attracted radio and, later, television transmitting towers and stations. Birmingham Public Library Archives; photographer: Watson McAlexander.

of children, the big man on the mountain has taken on morbid meaning.

So, less than a decade after the great Roman god of the forge — intended from creation for the 1904 St. Louis World's Fair to represent Birmingham's essential metals industry — finally reached suitable position, the basic symbolism was obscured. "Light for Life" may have been a worthy cause, but it has completely compromised the landmark's integrity. Vulcan without the object he has just forged is simply not Vulcan.

INTO THE 50s

In 1953, *Vulcan's Tour Map of Birmingham*, sponsored by the Alabama Motorists Association, became part of a promotion for visitation to Vulcan Park and other Birmingham sites. Shown just west of Vulcan on the Red Mountain crest now were the antennas of what was identified as "Radio Park" and The Club, sites made accessible by a new road branching off from the one leading up to Vulcan Park.

A report on the tour promotion in the *Birmingham Post-Herald*, August 31, 1953, noted that approximately 234,000 people visited Vulcan Park the previous year. This estimated number included out-of-state visitors said to range from 30 to 40 percent. Numbers were great enough and trips by car increasing fast enough that an additional lane up the mountain was added and expanded parking areas built where there had been walking trails. A number of WPA stone features were demolished for these alterations.

Vulcan's 50th birthday in 1954 passed with little fanfare, though the occasion was noted in a brief feature charting his history published in *This Week, The Sunday Magazine*, a national newspaper supplement.

By the late 1950s, schemes to expand tourism potential at Vulcan were being put forward. One proposal generated by theater operator R. Norris Hadaway and illustrated by cartoonist Charles Brooks called for a theme experience including "fantasy land" boat rides through the abandoned Valley View Mine west of Vulcan and an underground cyclorama on the history of iron. One drawing included a monorail, foreshadowing a proposal to come.

A small report in *The Birmingham News*, June 21, 1959, announced that the Vulcan monument would be closed for about a month due to needed repairs. Questions about the supports for the observation platform had been raised, and steps also needed repair. As the years went on, Vulcan began to suffer from water damage, graffiti and general wear and tear.

Vulcan Company Names

Popularity of Vulcan as a name for local businesses jumped when Vulcan was placed atop Red Mountain. Through the 1930s, not more than four companies, listed in the city directory, used Vulcan in their names. That number went to nine in 1940, 16 in 1950 and peaked at 31 in 1960. In 1990 there were 13 uses (including two apartment buildings) named after Vulcan. The city-based Vulcan Materials Co., listed in Fortune 500, was not named after Birmngham's Vulcan.

VULCAN GOES MOD

It is not clear why Vulcan was allowed to decline or how much, in fact, the once-heralded attraction *had* declined. There are indications the park was simply considered out of date.

A rendering of the 1969 master plan for a modernized Vulcan Park includes vast new parking, spiral ramps and other features including a monorail. The tower has new cladding, an expanded base, an exposed elevator and an enclosed observation platform. Birmingham Public Library Archives; photographer: John Acton.

This was a period when modernization always seemed the thing to do. There were legitimate arguments for elevator access and other improvements, but the overarching impetus seemed to be that Vulcan could attract more visitors if given major new features.

In October 1964, the Vulcan Park Improvement Commission, Inc., was incorporated as a nonprofit group "to promote the development and betterment of cultural and civic activities within the greater Birmingham area, including, but not limited to, the further development of Vulcan Park and the statue of Vulcan as a leading landmark and tourist attraction of the Birmingham area."

By 1969, the Birmingham firm of Elliott and Bradford, Architects, completed a master plan for Vulcan Park. Very much of its time, the design brought a futuristic look to Vulcan and his setting highlighted by a monorail proposed

This view of the 1969 plan shows a parking deck and a hotel with an anvil-shaped restaurant on the roof. Birmingham Public Library Archives; photographer: John Acton.

to extend from Vulcan along the face of Red Mountain and down the then-developing Red Mountain Expressway to link up with the zoo and botanical gardens. Spiral ramps, vastly expanded parking, new cladding for the tower supporting Vulcan and a new observation deck would all but eliminate the WPA stonework.

In addition, the north slope of the ridge facing the city, described as the "slide area," would get an eight-level, 700-car parking deck with a motel and restaurant incorporated in the design. This was handled as a separate element, possibly built by private enterprise.

The same study included, but did not further develop or include in estimates, the earlier proposal for the Valley View Mine underground experience. As a bow to Vulcan, it was noted that the wedge-shaped restaurant perched on the roof of the parking deck "has been designed in the stylized shape of an anvil."

With a total cost estimated (very roughly) at $10 million, initial phases of the project were to be built in 18 months and completed in time for the city's centennial in 1971.

The Greater Birmingham Ministerial Association opposed the plan, stating that "Red Mountain should be saved for beauty and dignity, not used as an amusement park" (The white marble sculpture of Brother Bryan, which had been set below Vulcan on a terrace named "Prayer Point," has since been moved back to Five Points South.).

Comparison of Vulcan overlooking Birmingham c. 1965, before modern features were added (above), with the aerial view taken by National Park Service photographer Jet Lowe as part of a 1993 survey (below), makes clear how changes to the tower overwhelm the statue. 1965 view, Birmingham Public Library Archives; 1993 view, Historic American Engineering Record; photographer: Jet Lowe.

While the monorail, massive parking deck, motel and restaurant were dropped, the modernization project moved ahead with the support of then-Mayor George Seibels, Jr., and a bond issue (estimated by various sources to be from $1 million to $3 million) was earmarked for the work.

The 1969-71 modernization included demolition of the original restrooms, the stone fountain cascade and the museum at the base of the tower. New concrete ramps and overlooks physically cut off and visually obscured the original WPA stone steps and terraces. The stone-clad tower was sheathed in white polished marble affixed to a metal framework bolted through the stone to the concrete frame within the tower. At the base of the tower, a flared anodized aluminum roof covered a new and larger structure. An external elevator was added, as was an expanded, enclosed observation deck.

The executed part of the design is, indeed, modern — and flawed. Thickening of the tower, addition of the outside elevator shaft plus larger enclosures above and below have created a massive form that visually overwhelms the statue (see contrasting silhouette drawings). Views of Vulcan from the site are now made difficult and, with a solid roof overhead, visitors have no chance to view Vulcan up close. Though the most contrived features, like the spiral ramps, were not built, expanses of concrete walks and plazas overwhelm the natural setting.

All in all, the fine relationship between the original slim, stone tower, the walks and fountains and the rugged natural character of the site, so fully realized in 1939, has been lost. The modernization of Vulcan Park paralleled

Silhouette profiles of the two views on the previous page emphasize the diminution of Vulcan. 1965 view; Birmingham Public Library Archives; 1993 view; Historic American Engineering Record; photographer: Jet Lowe.

Two photographs documenting Vulcan Park in 1993 contrast the more natural stonework and landscape remaining from the WPA period (1936) with the expansive paving and formal planting beds created as part of the 1969-71 renovations. Historic American Engineering Record-National Park Service; photographer: Jet Lowe.

the blank facades applied to so many of Birmingham's (and indeed, America's) buildings during this period — under similar good intentions and with the same unfortunate results.

It is ironic that Vulcan and Vulcan Park were added to the National Register of Historic Places on July 6, 1976, not long after the site's grace and character had been modernized away.

LOST AND FOUND

Even as these slick new improvements were being built, diversions for potential Vulcan visitors were developing.

Though there was a spurt of attendance at the remodeled Vulcan Park with its city observation deck, the construction of Interstate 65 as the new primary north-south route through the city (in phases during the late 1960s and 1970s) and completion of U.S. 280 through Red Mountain (by 1970) meant the destination was no longer on a major route. Vulcan became and remains, not easy for visitors to find, even while the statue can be seen from afar.

Denying the "Moon"

"I remember walking up the steps and looking up trying to decide whether Vulcan had on pants!" recalls one visitor taken there as a child. Well, he doesn't, and his bare buttocks have generated shock and mirth from the beginning. But interestingly, this fact never seems to have been recorded in public.

Moretti, of course, did not intend to shock or generate snickers. In the Italian Renaissance tradition reaching back to the 15th century, the human body was considered the greatest expression of God's creation. Sculpting or painting it nude or only partially draped was, therefore, a legitimate function of art.

Interestingly, this obvious fact about Vulcan seems

never to have been mentioned in print or public comment. None of MacKnight's published letters concluded, "P.S. He has a bare fanny, and it looks great!" When the *Birmingham Age-Herald* ran a photograph of his freshly cast buttocks on March 16, 1904, the title over it read, "ONE SECTION OF VULCAN," and the cutline beneath said, "Iron casting of body from waist to point between thigh and knees."

And in Birmingham Publishing Co.'s 1938 booklet, *Birmingham's Vulcan*, the paragraph run just opposite a fine photograph of the colossus on his new column taken from the parking lot notes, "Vulcan's brawny back is viewed by those who approach the statue from the south."

It is only in our candid, modern times that the gift shop offers a popular t-shirt for sale with a tight rear view labeled, "Moon Over Homewood," the latter being the first suburb to the south.

Documented Statistics

As part of the Historic American Engineering Record documentation of the statue, monument and park, consultant Richard Anderson calculated the dimensions, working from historic photographs and U.S.G.S. maps.

Statue Height: 56 feet at the fair; post fair; 53.5 feet due to loss of original right arm and spear point

Pedestal Height: 123.5 feet

Valley-to-Mountain-Top Height: 382 feet

Valley to Tip of Vulcan's Spear Point: 560 feet

And, too, the welcome addition of other cultural and recreational attractions in the Birmingham metropolitan area provided competition. Though it was still the best site open to the general public to overlook the city, anyone just driving within view could say they'd seen Vulcan. (He had been painted the color of iron ore under Mayor David Vann's administration, a move many thought appropriate and that others complained made the statue less visible at night.)

While Birmingham Parks and Recreation maintained Vulcan Park in generally good condition, the facility became dated. Vulcan mainly got attention when the neon tubes in his traffic safety light had to be replaced (Annual visitation in 1994 was 83,305 with an admission fee of $1). Even so, when the Birmingham Historical Society sponsored schoolchildren's drawings of Birmingham, Vulcan would nearly always appear – often not exactly where you'd expect and always rendered at wildly varied scales.

The first move to reassess Vulcan in his setting came from the neighborhood just below. In 1979, the Five Points South Neighborhood Association helped fund, with its city allocation, a *Vulcan/Red Mountain Linear Park Master Plan* by Charles W. Greiner & Associates, Inc., landscape architects. Though realized work was limited to a new recreational trail and overlook below the park, a nature-historic trail to Valley View Mine using the old mineral railroad right-of-way was put forward in the plan.

A few years later, Mayor Richard Arrington expressed interest in developing a restaurant and conference center at Vulcan Park and architect Charles Moss prepared preliminary plans for 34,000 square feet of new space plus a 200-space parking deck. Again, the Five Points South neighborhood and many other community organizations got involved with a public forum. The Birmingham Historical Society created a Vulcan committee at about the same time.

At the urging of the neighborhood, the Birmingham Area Chamber of Commerce established a task force to consider the future of Vulcan Park, coming up with a strategic plan in 1988. While not a physical plan, this was a listing of priorities that included restaurant and meeting space plus suggestions of "additional programming and displays to attract visitors and lengthen stay including community support group, Vulcan observatory, multi-media historical center, expanded hiking trail, mine

entrance exhibit, amphitheater/outdoor performance space, access and parking."

A Greater Vulcan Society was formed and a series of studies pursuing these ideas culminated in a late-1990 master plan prepared by architects Adams Design Associates and landscape architects Nimrod Long and Associates. The design program was more modest (meeting space, but no restaurant or amphitheater). Most importantly, this plan called for removal of the modern cladding on the tower, replacement of the present observation deck with a glass-roofed painted steel version (Eiffel Tower-inspired), recreation of the stone cascades and other changes looking back to the WPA period. There was no monorail in the renderings.

This drawing of Vulcan Park is both documentary and interpretive. It captures in one image the statue of Vulcan and its symbolic placement in a prominent park setting over the iron ore vein that supplied Birmingham's early industry. Historic American Engineering Record-National Park Service; illustrator: Richard K. Anderson, Jr., 1993.

A series of photogrammetric aerial views were taken as part of documentation in 1993 for use in executing measured drawings of the statue. Historic American Engineering Record-National Park Service; photographer: Jet Lowe.

Clearly, the new emphasis on historic preservation that had seen removal of scores of modern coverups from city center buildings during the 1980s was at work. Meanwhile, the statue itself, suffering from age and structural accommodations made when he was anchored to his Red Mountain tower, needed attention. Studies dealing with Vulcan, the site and historic interpretation would soon gain focus.

RESTORING VULCAN

Problems with Vulcan cracking and with the concrete poured inside him to help anchor him to his pedestal have been studied with various solutions proposed. This photograph appeared on the front page of The Birmingham News, *March 3, 1995, with an article headlined, "Vulcan Needs a Big Fix."* The Birmingham News; *photographer: Frank Couch.*

The concrete poured into Vulcan up to his shoulders to help anchor him to his new perch in the late 1930s was effective in a make-do way. He was, and still is, stable, with metal rods extending from the concrete tower cap 10 feet into his legs. But concrete expands and contracts at a different rate than cast iron, and the concrete tends to trap moisture with long-term deleterious effects on the iron plates and their connections. Vulcan is slowly cracking up.

Leaching of lime through these seams became more and more evident and, in 1991, the City hired Law Engineering Industrial Services to study the problem. About the same time, Robinson Iron, a foundry based in Alexander City, Alabama, and nationally known for restoration and recasting of historic ironwork, suggested taking Vulcan down, piece by piece, restoring whatever needed attention, and re-installing him on a metal armature anchored to the tower.

The Law study showed Vulcan to be in essentially sound condition, considering his age and what had been done to him, and recommended a method that might be used to secure the cracks (cast iron cannot be welded). But this would not correct the essential problem, a conclusion supported by Nick Veloz, a specialist in conservation of monument sculpture with the National Park Service retained by the City for an assessment. Veloz also argued that the historic open top of Vulcan's head be left open. Since it is virtually impossible to keep moisture out of hollow outdoor sculptures, they should be allowed to drain and ventilate freely. Restored properly, Vulcan would last indefinitely, Veloz reported, noting that an exterior cast iron sculpture in India erected some 3,000 years ago remains in good condition, today.

During this same period, a survey of sites related to a proposed Birmingham Industrial

Heritage District identified the potential of Vulcan and Vulcan Park as both a National Historic Landmark and as an interpretive center for the district. As part of this multi-year study, the Historic American Engineering Record (HAER), a Washington-based division of the National Park Service, prepared measured drawings, documentary photographs and text on Vulcan and his setting at the time of the WPA project, and did a similar assessment of the nearby Valley View Red Ore Mine which operated from 1904 to 1924.

Separately, the concept of a trail between Vulcan Park and Valley View Mine was revisited with a 1993 study and plan by Nimrod Long and Associates, commissioned by the City as part of a successful ISTEA (Intermodal Surface Transportation Efficiency Act) request. Restoration and interpretation of the WPA-era improvements to Vulcan Park were recommended.

In August 1993, Mayor Richard Arrington appointed a Vulcan Task Force including representatives from his office, the City's parks department, planning and engineering department,

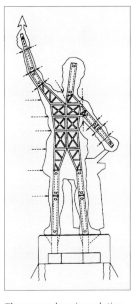

The comprehensive solution for the statue is to take it down in pieces, remove the concrete, restore parts that need it and reinstall them on a steel armature mounted to the tower. Robinson Iron, 1994.

This watercolor rendering suggests how Vulcan Park would appear if returned to the character of the WPA period. With an interior elevator, the tower would, once again, have its slender profile and stonework exposed. The landscape would defer to the natural setting and views of Vulcan would be improved. A new visitor center to tell Vulcan's story and the history of the city would be constructed at the site. Birmingham Historical Society; watercolor by Bob Moody, Moody/Sprague, 1995.

Vulcan becomes the center of attention each July 4 with fireworks highlighting him against the sky. With restoration and new interpretive features, the venerable landmark has an important role to play every day. Photographer: John C. Acton.

and the Birmingham Historical Society, to review various studies and recommendations for Vulcan. The task force recommended the full restoration of the statue and the park.

WHITHER VULCAN?

Over these many years, now past 90, Vulcan has seen his triumphs and his troubles. The creation of the colossal iron man was a bold act for a young, on-the-make industrial city, its leaders and its skilled foundrymen. Sculptor Moretti's conception and rapid execution were equally heroic, producing a work of monumental art on a timetable few would have attempted. After his rather sad decades at the state fairgrounds, even then fondly remembered by generations, Vulcan was given his perfect site and prime condition in the late 1930s.

The evidence is compelling that Vulcan and his setting should be returned to the grace and dignity of that era. Tower stonework is virtually intact beneath the modern skin, and the site can be at least partially re-naturalized. This could not be an exact restoration to 1939. There still needs to be an elevator (this time inside the shaft), and a tiny observation balcony won't suffice (something halfway between the original and the current one would work). And an expanded museum/interpretive function would require appropriate space.

But with the right balance struck, a fully restored Vulcan and an appropriately renovated park will assume fresh vitality as a symbol of the city and region. American cities with colossal public sculpture are a handful, and no other place has Vulcan. Few cities have such a breathtaking natural overlook so close to their heart as Vulcan Park. As this book, we hope, makes clear, Vulcan and his times make an intriguing story. And Vulcan can help tell the history of the city at his feet for residents and visitors alike.

Vulcan, Roman god of the forge and Birmingham's unforgettable giant on the hill, needs friends, again.

Key Dates

Oct. 13, 1903
Commercial Club chooses Vulcan to represent Birmingham.

Nov. 24, 1903
Moretti commissioned to sculpt the colossal iron man.

Jan.-Feb. 1904
Full-size plaster casts poured at St. Stephen's Church, Passaic, NJ.

March 12-May 7, 1904
Birmingham Steel and Iron foundry casts the Iron Man of Sloss No. 2 Pig Iron.

May 1-Nov. 30, 1904
Vulcan as Alabama's exhibit in the Palace of Mines and Metallurgy, St. Louis World's Fair.

October 1906-1935
Vulcan at the Alabama State Fairgrounds.

1935-1939
Kiwanis Club spearheads public-private campaign to build the Red Mountain monument, museum and park.

1968-1971
Vulcan Park modernized for Birmingham's Centennial Celebration.

1993
The Historic American Engineering Record-National Park Service documents the statue and park as a possible "National Historic Landmark" site.

1995
Birmingham plans for the full restoration of the statue and park.

ACKNOWLEDGEMENTS

This publication was made possible by many individuals and institutions:

Philip A. Morris, author

Marjorie L. White, editor and research coordinator

Scott Fuller, icon graphics, design

Marjorie Lee White, Chris Dorsey, Carol Slaughter, Walton Eagan, Amy Hamilton, Brenda Howell, Bill Jones, researchers

Stewart Dansby, Joe Strickland, James White, copy editors

Assistance with research and photography:

Don Veasey, Marvin Whiting, Don Baggett, Elizabeth Swift, Birmingham Public Library, Department of Archives and Manuscripts

Yvonne Crumpler, Grace Reid, Ron Julian, Birmingham Public Library, Southern History Department

Danny Dorrah, Danny Cusick, Becky Scarborough, Birmingham Public Library, Government Documents Department

Dr. Robert Kapsch, Eric DeLony, Richard O'Connor, Craig Strong, Jet Lowe, Historic American Engineering Record-National Park Service, Washington, DC

Catharine Stuart, Kiwanis Club

John Acton, photographer

Deborah Brown, Missouri Historical Society, St. Louis, MO

Mark Anders, New York Public Library, New York, NY

Walter Wojtowicz, Chicago Public Library, Chicago, IL

Barry Mareno, Statue of Liberty, National Park Service, New York, NY

Hugh Terry, William Stanley Hoole Special Collection Library, Tuscaloosa, AL

Prints and Drawing Division, Library of Congress, Washington, DC

Sherry Birk, Curator, Prints and Drawings Collection, The Octagon, The Museum of the American Architectural Foundation, Washington DC

Flavia Alaya, Patterson, NJ

Father Stephen Mustos, St. Stephen's Church, Passaic, NJ

Richard K. Anderson, Jr., Columbia, SC

Walter Karcheski, John Woodman Higgins Armory, Worcester, MA

George Thompson, Vulcan historian

Eddie Mae Johnson, Birmingham Parks & Recreation Board

Dr. Samuel Stayer, Birmingham-Southern College

Joe Holley, Alabama Highway Department

Gwyn Turner, Demoplis, AL

Alvin Hudson

Will Dickey

John O'Hagan

ACKNOWLEDGEMENTS

Assistance with promotion and distribution:

Southern Progress Corporation, Kenner Patton, Karen Mitchell, Shirley Wilson

Bruno's and Vincent's Market, Joe Bruno, Catherine Byrd, Lisa Caldwell, the managers and employees of all Birmingham area stores

National Bank of Commerce, John Holcomb, Kim Moore.

Project Coordination:

Members of the Birmingham Historical Society Trustees' Vulcan Committee: David Herring, Chairman; Hugh Rushing; Philip Morris; Michael Mills; Marjorie White

Members of the Society's Vulcan Promotion Committee: Stewart Dansby, Hugh Rushing, Carolanne Griffith-Roberts.

11-43

11/6-43